Dragonflies Surrender

by

PENGUIN SCOTT

I hope enjoy these poems.

Penguin Scott

Dragonflies Surrender
Cover art by Penguin Scott

Copyright © 2023 Penguin Scott

Any persons in this book, if real, are now fictional characters, their likenesses have been altered, dramatized, enhanced, or detracted from. Any semblance to real people is coincidental and unintended. All works are original to the author. Any similarities to works of others is coincidental or inspired by these works.

All rights reserved. No part of this publication may be reproduced, distributed, or transmitted in any form or means without the prior written permission of the copyright holder, except in the case of brief quotations embodied in articles and reviews with credits to the author. For permission requests, write to the publisher, addressed "Attention Permission Coordinator," at the email below.

Published by Penguin Scott / Flying Rockhopper Press Publishing
ISBN: 978-1-312-79424-5

authorpenguinscott@gmail.com
www.penguinscott.com

Mother's Day 2014

You're special in the morning
You're special all day through
Your words of advice and caring
Brighten all you do
You're a goddess known in Heaven
I know this to be true
Thanks for being my mommy
Forever I love you

This book I dedicate to her
Always the brightest star in my universe

<u>Seven</u>

I stole an eraser from a red-haired girl
And tossed it onto the roof of our school
Did so on other's behest
Stole a kid's sandwich during recess
Maybe I thought it would make me seem cool

I felt bad before I got caught
Then teacher asked me a question
If others jumped off a bridge, would I follow the lot
I said no to the suggestion
Jumping off a bridge might get me killed
For tossing an eraser I'll only be grilled

Speaking of grilled she next inquired
During class why did you sneak that boy's sandwich
I was hungry, and what I desired
I never found out which kid snitched

That night I was asked about my day
Thinking quickly I switched the subject up
Some boys at school used the words I can't say
I'm sure hungry, when can we sup?

...

I got away with my little scheme
But so few times it would seem
The little white lies we told in younger days
I guess we all go through such a troublesome phase

The things I did and the words I'd say
Sure come back to haunt one day
They raise up tall, I feel ashamed
I own them all and have since been tamed
Always wondered what I'd grow up to be
The hard lessons learned now honor me

Snoopykins

My grandparents had a cat named snoopy
Snoopy was an indoor/outdoor cat
He made his intention to get inside clear
by attaching himself firmly to the screen door at eye level
Human eye level
His meow was a deep baritone that couldn't be ignored
Let me in
NOW
Snoopy was a lover
Snoopy supplied the fleas that kept me scratching
all summer long
Snoopy died and soon after I came to visit
That's when I found out
Goodbye Snoopy
Hello Buffy

Lampasas, Texas On A Hot Afternoon

I met her in Lampasas
She was pruning trees under the sun in oppressive Texas heat
We spent time talking in the shade, she and I, as a few cars crept by and music of the cicadas played
The shade should have been cooling, but it felt like it was a hundred and one
The pecan trees rustled gently in what I would hardly call a breeze
The Texas Hill Country breeze that simply moves the heat around making me wonder why summer can't be more like winter, when the wind flows so freely and briskly
The rustling pecan trees with their sweet, nutty and buttery kernels were much shorter way back when she was a girl, I'm sure she would agree
Her social circle was shrinking as her age climbed higher, so she loved the chance to chat with anyone willing to listen

A bit more fussy, I love to chat with any affable person as long as they have something interesting to say
This was where my grandmother was born and raised by a doctor and his wife and I wondered if maybe she knew someone in my family, if not at least familiar with the family name
They had lived somewhere on this street, in a large wooden house much like, if not, hers
She was neighborly, cheerful, spry, unfamiliar with my clan, but she could count the times she's been to Austin by the number of shoes she had inside her closet. I never found out how often she went

Memories

I have vague memories of places I've been
    When I was three
    A picture window
    A bite to eat
    With people I don't know
A place in my mind that I can barely see after all this time
    Where was this?
    Why was I there?
    Who are those strangers?
    Where are they now?
    Are they even still around?
These are a few vague memories of things I'll never know

Corpus, Back In The Day

Walking to the store
From a house near the end of the street
Hear the sound of cars rushing past
Holding grandfather's hand
Two fingers in my palms
Me on one side
My cousin on the other

Fishing off the T-heads
In the warm bay waters
Not about the catch
But being with Paw

Butter stored in Tupperware always left out on the table
A lazy Susan with sugar, pepper juice, and salt
Dish rags hang on the oven handle
Empty cups on the counter
To be used again
They grew up in the depression
Thrifty was their way

Old toys in a box on Paw's closet floor
Belonged to my father, my uncle, my older cousin
That tiger puppet with plastic head,
The yellow race car that looked like a banana,

...

The football game plugged in that buzzed the players
around on a green tin playing field and sports fans
displayed on thick cardboard bleachers
B'zzzzzzzzz

Memaw looks sad today
Now that Paw has passed
So many years together
Soon she won't remember his name

What I'd give to have it all back

Grandmother

From the halo up on top of her head to her sweet vanilla toes
She's greater yet than sliced bread
She's the fragrance of a rose
When I was young I gave her a name
My sweet Itsy Bitsy
And now that she has notoriety and fame
We just call her Itsy
We love to get together
A family as one
For Itsy we sing and cheer
Ninety-three times around the sun
Grandmother is so dear
Itsy so missed by her eldest grandson

Memorial Day

With dew on my feet and clouds rolling overhead, the sun, then shade, then sun again, refusing to relieve the oppressive, muggy humidity, which permitted me to question the sanity of my being there, but only briefly. This was a mission.

The shrill of bagpipes wailed somewhere nearby while innumerable American flags proudly flanked the winding, black-top road of the National Cemetery. More flags waved from each simple, white head stone, lined in military-precision, and swaying atop a Houston ladder truck, with rungs extended sunward, was the largest flag of them all.

Throngs of spectators to the somber ceremony for their loved ones filled here and there, some carrying flags, many with flowers, others wearing vests adorned with military patches, medals, and numerous folk visiting loved ones interred under the lush, green carpet of grass- perhaps the greenest in all of Houston.

And there was I, in compliment to the spectacle, honoring my grandfather, a World War II Navy Veteran who served our country on the USS St. Louis in the Pacific Theater, inhumed in 2000, and expressing gratitude for
all those who served our nation and are memorialized on this sacred ground, under passing clouds, a rising sun, and large flag aflare atop a shiny, red fire truck. Poppy, who I sorely miss and still deeply love, thank you for protecting our country.

Borger

My breath is the Texas high plains wind.
My fondness sways as the tall grass where the canyons bend
My heart beats like the rhythm of the pump jack churning crude oil from majestic Texas ground
Little Stinky Borger
My spirit you found

Where manners are common and pickups are king
Where The Bulldogs are depicted, praised, laud, and sing
In the shadow of refineries that light up at night, as the large cities of the east coast might
Hearing the collision of train cars connecting in the rail yard, and strange wafting odors of petroleum refineries of Phillips 66
High winds, twisters, and rolling thunder when lightning strobing the night skies leaves me transfixed

Among arid canyons of the Texas Panhandle
Shaded by cactus, wheatgrass, juniper, and yucca
Playground of songbirds, mule deer, rabbits, and the horny toad
Ladies and cowboys, and pipeliners abode

I am home
I am eternal
Borger, Texas
Hold me like you have since I was just a small boy
My grounded retreat with style and joy
Discovering the glory of youth, snow, and solitaire
With love
And family and friends who care
Never leave my mind, Bigger, Better Borger
As if you ever could, or would ever dare

Like Mom Used To Do

I was well on my way until I saw my own reflection in the well of sorrow over which I am thrust
Now I'm stuck in a rut and can't get up
I'm burning up and blowing by life
This voice fills my head dawn to dusk

It's taken a lifetime to grapple with how I feel about my path in life
All the memories that haunt me play in my mind like the black and whites, which Mom played on TV when I was a small boy
On a rainy Sunday afternoon in the darkened living room
Curtains drawn with a just a crack to see the rain
While Mom popped kernels of corn in an air popper that was the color of avocados
She was always so calm and caring in how she moved
Style and grace I rarely see in life

Wondering how many days Mom felt this way and wishing I had someone
the way she had someone to share a day like this
When the rain matched her mood at the end of a long week

She always had me for those times she craved comfort
Cherry turnovers hot out of the oven, old movies, tomato
soup with a grilled cheese, and me

And with warm memories as such
I climb out of the well
Feeling less stuck I manage to stand up
But life still blows by in a rush and most likely always will
It's up to me to pause
Take an intermission
Even if still at a loss as to how I feel

Maybe I should plop down
In the middle of a mid-week day
Pull the curtains closed
To watch old Mabel Normand movies on the TV
And eat a large bowl of popcorn
Melted butter, salt, and all

Turkey Talk

I walked into the kitchen to find my mother and grandmother preparing a turkey for the big Thanksgiving meal. The pinkish bird, sat naked in a large pan—my grandmother poking and prodding at it, as if it might start to cook on its own.

Mom was leaning over the counter with the family cookbook opened in front of her face. Itsy can't remember from year to year how to prepare it. "You know, when you only cook a bird once a year, you forget how to do it," Itsy said in her defense.

Mom agreed, saying, "I know. One year I cooked a bird upside down." I asked Mom how it turned out. "Fine," she said, "but when I went to carve it, it was really difficult—I was saying, 'there's no meat on this at all!'"

We all laughed, but then Mom got back to business and read the directions from her cookbook to her mother out loud.

The next step was to coat the skin with oil. "I thought I used butter," said Itsy. Mom shot back, "But butter will burn." "Oh, you *are* right. I'm so glad I have such smart girls," said Itsy of Mom and her two younger sisters, neither of whom were in the kitchen assisting.

I broke in, "But she cooked a bird upside down! How smart can a person be to cook a bird upside down?"

Mom looked shocked and then glared at me, as I stood with my shit-eating smile. "You better not tell anyone," she said.

And to support her statement on how smart her daughter was, her mother said, "At least she learned her lesson."

And so went one of the best Thanksgivings of all.

A Day For Mom

You carried me and brought me here
When I'm sad you wipe my tear
I see the strength inherited from you
Your teachings are in all things that I do
The foundation you built still stands quite solidly
My home you inspired is top quality
In you my friends are so very amazed
At the character in the man that you raised
With a hug and a smile it is the day I get to say
I wish for you a happy and bright Mother's Day

Twenty Years Later

The first time I saw them
I was gifted a view from the top
The second time I saw them
Was a magical photo op
From just behind the wing
An amazing scene
Taken 12 months before what was never foreseen

Our country thrust in hell
When those towers fell
What started on a beautiful day
Would unite us together
Memories might slowly decay
The scars can last forever

It still tears me apart
My poor little broken heart
As the years advance may the virtues of love to us impart

...And perhaps a little more understanding

Challenger

The cabin crew survived until it hit the water. That's what they now say.
I remember where I was that cold January day.
I can't imagine the ride down.
  Panic.
  Fear.
  Anger.

  ◊

  Acceptance.
  Sadness.
  Peace.
The sax played no more. The soccer ball returned to earth but perchance to float among the heavens at last, it's purpose later met in testament to those who fell.
The lessons learned are
taught no more.

I heard a noise. A moment of silence.
A bell rang. Seven tolls and the state of the union delayed.
Yes.
I remember it all- that cold January day.

Through The Salt

And he couldn't see
From the salt in his eyes

And yet through those tears
He could figure out why
He hurt so much

Grief

My heart broke into so many pieces
It's lost inside me
Filtered down through my dejected body
Little bits stuck here and there
Little pieces in my toes
If only I had thought to keep a spare

My heart broke
And has left a hole
I let out a weep
My mouth opened
I was every bit of flustered
But I was unable to scream
A pitiful whimper is all I could muster

My heart broke and it tasted like salt
The torrid pungency of my tears assault

You were my greatest treasure
Taken from me too soon
And when it happened
Part of me was taken, too
So my heart broke
What ever am I to do

Mary

The angel of my life
Grew wings today and flew away

My best friend now soaring on the wind
To new fields of green
With new dreams to dream
Left me behind now my angel on my mind
Knowing that one day we'll again make a team

Redwoods

Tracie is among the redwood trees
In a forest fresh with wooded breeze
Her smile lights up ever so bright
Making a most magical sight

We'll sit and eat blackberries so sweet
We'll warm ourselves by fireside heat
They come from near and so far
They come to nibble from her cookie jar

Tracie was so warm and caring
Knew all about giving and sharing
Her time with us was not long enough
Without her here, the going is rough

But when we feel alone and sad
Because we miss the times we had
Just close your eyes and welcome the breeze
For Tracie's alight in the redwood trees

Falling

I am forever falling
The hopeless romantic in me
We catch eyes and I am hooked

Falling for you
Blindly
Until I find a shell of you
Gone as fast as I found you

They always fade
Growing cold under a worn out spell

And I've let myself down again
Hopes dashed on jagged shore
Expectations always overgrown
Turning into dust
Fading away

Until I meet the next one

I am forever falling
Damned hopeless romantic in me

Delicate Web

Is there anything more delicate than a spider's web?
Than me and you?
Than the exhaustive hell but to fortify our bond?
Than your prolonged absence while I strive to decipher
my love for you?

An invention unequaled, the two of us
      Ageless
            Exquisite
                 Elegant
Entirely in my mind.

You allege I'm the beauty, still you fill the screen- splendor exposed.
Complacent, I'll be your audience.
Single in purpose to receive your adoration.

My beguiling, lovely, beautiful you.
Your brilliance governs my existence, for I am the fool.

Hopelessly yours and stricken by you.
In the delicate web entangling us two.

Low Priority

Swept under the rug
No harm to be done
No feelings to be felt
To get in the way
Of your higher priorities
I'll try again later

Adjust

If you withdraw
Go into yourself

It's not so dark
Once your eyes adjust

Filbert's Tapping

There's a bird at my window
Tapping so sweetly
Wanting to come in
Each morning
Like the sun rising again

Sweet Adelie could it be you
Stuck in my heart
Trying to get out
Every night
When the stars are all out

There's a cat caressing my feet
Purring rapidly
Like you used to do
Every day
You loved me that way

Dragonfly drifting so softly
Then landing on me
Pulling me out
Every way
Leaving me without doubt
That's what the circle is all about

Needing Sad Songs

Sometimes I listen to the sad songs
Sung by buttery voices
Forlorn and melancholy

The sad songs that know us so well
Recognize our pain because pain is shared universally

We need a good cry to cleanse the internal damage and bring clarity
Disrupt the maze of life for a time and replace confusion with closure and parity

We need a cry for emotional re-set
A deluge of water to clear the spirit- the rubbish of fret
All those feelings felt in so many places by so many faces

So I listen to the sad songs
Sung by velvety voices
Saying
Know me ... know my pain universally
And then go about my day with better feelings displaying

Cede

I'm not afraid to die
        It's pain that gets my undivided scrutiny
So I ask her to take me softly
        But she leaves me to roam
So I roam

<u>Spring</u>

What makes you say rainy days are gloomy?

There's no gloom when one remembers the sun is still as radiant as ever, high up in the sky now crowded with clouds.

Can't have flowers without a few hours of rain.

Dream Journal

I used to keep my dreams in a journal
But I stopped

The dreams were particularly vibrant
Such beauty that words elude my mind
The concepts revealed difficult to grasp in the light of day

    Many moments spent
    Line after line
    Setting up the scene
    The splendor of the dream

        But I stopped
        This shouldn't be read into
        Over analyzed
        Or even let throe

On The Mountainside

While visiting Mom in her mountainside home in Colorado, I hiked up above the house into the wilderness of Red Mountain, and found a magical space. I knew it was magical the moment I happened upon it. There was an outcropping of rocks at 11,600 feet that created a fortress of solitude sized for one—a perfect place. Each time I visited, I hiked up into the wilderness. Mom would ask each time, "Are going to climb up to your favorite spot?" It should not have been easy to find a second time. Or a third. Or fourth, fifth and sixth. I always found it, without landmarks or trails, across a patch of fallen rocks, up and up, a new path made each time. I rested between the rocks that rosse from the mountain as if protecting me from the world. I've spent hours in this space, over many visits: meditating, in ritual, listening, dancing, observing. Mom no longer lives on Red Mountain. Yet, this is where I go. The rocks, the trees, the gentle mountain breeze. When things get rough and go awry. This is where I go when I need to cry...laugh...find strength...simply escape. A wind blowing down the valley in no hurry. An echo, but of what? A snap. A fallen tree perhaps? A rock falling off a ledge? No matter. As if I'm really there, I'm in this place where I go when I need to be anywhere but in this world. In my mind. At any time when I need to be *present*. It will be waiting for me   Always.

Through The Window

I felt my way in the dark
to find an open window
I couldn't see, yet my spirit felt free.

Dreams see me tumbling through the night
My heart beating rapidly
Pounding within me
To craft a custom dream
where I hoped to find the escape I need

Through the window was a connection
to a here and now
from a there and then

I thought my journey ended
But I was wrong
So I circled around again
as I have those times before
Maybe soon I'd learn my lesson
With understanding, the window
can become a door.

...

In moonlight was a circle;
Within it was me.
I lit a tapered candle.
Beat a goat-skinned drum.
Lifted my soul and hung it
high on a canyon wall.

The image of the ego
I labored to leave behind
Was no longer with me.

Until in the circle, I couldn't let go.
But once in the circle stood
I learned that I honestly could.

Ohma Gods

There's something I need you to know
The Ohma gods are out of control
Think they are helping the misfit
Blind to the fear they emit

Lay us to rest with the masses
Ohma gods making us anxious
Be it in boardrooms or in our classes
We are on the edge of creating a gem
Except
Ohma god this and Ohma god them

The Oma gods are trying to get us
Surely you know what that means
They will turn us all into nothing
Lickity split... so in their dreams

It's amazing what fear can breed
But before it does its infernal deed
There's something we should know

All was great without the Ohma gods
We don't need any of them now
I resist their dream killer
And it's getting harder to hold out

...

She's got a gun and she'll use it
Using her faith as a weapon
Shooting us with her beliefs
Our values differ, I reckon

This fear darkens and grows
At least until the whistle blows
Until then, we face insurmountable odds
In the vitriolic realm of the Ohma gods

And then when the whole world implodes
What topics will they confront?
When a small mind so speedily overloads
And the only things they've yet to hunt

Just what are the odds?
Are their fellow Ohma gods

Special

     You're so special
Must be careful not to hold you too close
Would be a shame
    To suffocate the feelings I'm sure you have
Maybe the glass is too thick
Or your head got in the way

     You're so special
What will be your best defense
Will you remember
    To check your feelings at the door
You covet what is important only to you
And internally hold a world so dear

     You're so special
Cannot commit to what it should take
But no, you're not fake
      Just too sightless to view that which
      before you imparts
Feelings unknown and strangers to your heart

...

      You're so special
And as you design us to suffer
   the shadows blocking your view
   With feelings so muted
Paranoid in the dreams of others
Such dreams your darkness casts askew

Candidate

Tiny little man
With hatred in his heart
Cling to your painted faith
Until Earth shall you part

Line up all your mindless believers
Who follow you through hell
They cling to your every word
Dismissing integrity's bell

Lie to us like no one else has
In the history of the race
Make us all believe
Your wickedly lying face

A monster is what you've created
In yourself and across our land
Shame shall befall us all
Our pride you have dis-banned

There are so many wonderful paths
That one may proudly follow

...

Yours is ghastly fertilized
With lies you make us swallow

I don't believe your way is best
I don't believe your faith
Stop preaching your spiteful nonsense
Such lies that you create

Travel Lust

I could fly to India, or even to Japan
I could journey anywhere and not need a plan
With travel lust sprouting from somewhere deep within
I'm always ready to travel, as long as turbines spin

To leap from this country and into the next
With no rhyme or reason I truly lack pretext
I simply love to travel, of this have no doubt
It's not the destination, but more about the route

Never in a hurry to reach a pathway's end
Amazing people all over the world soon to be a friend
I love the varied histories and the cultures that I find
Appreciating how it opens and broadens a growing mind

With conveyances at the ready I am eager to travel
In hopes that hidden pathways will magically unravel
From here I must leave to there I soon alight
As long as I keep moving, my future's looming bright

Annapolis

There's a house down on the Severn River shore. A warm home that I so adore.
I can see the capitol dome from atop my home- from the balcony up on the fourth floor.

I see an academy of young cadets graduating beneath the roar of blue and yellow jets.
I dine on crab from the Chesapeake Bay. I watch a thunderstorm at the end of the day.

With four stories and six levels; made of wood and glass and of metals, I love how the water of the Severn River makes my home sparkle and glimmer.

It warms my heart and soothes my soul. As this home helps to make me whole.

If home is where the heart is stored, then my heart lies upon the Severn shore.

Leaving California

Sixty-two East with Twentynine Palms behind me
Pink sunset air – a transcendental sight
Ranch houses beside squeaky wind mills turning in the breeze
Ahead – a blacktop highway, straight and narrow
No cars behind me
No cars ahead
The road is mine
It's getting dark so fast
Passing a moon lit valley among darkened, rugged mountains
There, the moon making a slow ascent
Luna halo; round, bright, and large
Leaving California now
Sweet sorrow
Thank you, dear friend and goodbye

Planes In Clouds

Planes in clouds
Soaring through the air
Planes so loud
They make me want to stare
       The engines roar
       Wings lift
       Rudders move
       Flight is swift

Planes in clouds
Passing overhead
Overcast shrouds
Infinitely spread
       Fluffy white
       Grey with rain
       Moving fast
       Cloudy bane

Planes in clouds
Off to foreign lands
Enthusiast wows
Lauding flight's demands
       Want to see
       Vision's naught
       Metal birds
       Hard to spot

Metal Birds

Engines whine, twist and whirl
Through the sky this bird shall hurl

Metal fuselage, metal wings
Metal birds are shiny things

Into the sky we now alight
Across the day into the night

From far away I now fly near
To be with you over here

I soon must go, I cannot stay
But I'll fly back again some day

Con Trails At Night

Con trails at night under the stars
Wispy, silvery, vapor under moon exposed
Streaking across the darkened sky
Beaming down twin lines in shadow
Isn't that neat?

Leading end with winking lights
Airliner so far ahead
Up high in the sky at night
The other end a vanishing point
A silvery slight
Marking the path of a journey's flight

Love to see...such a glorious sight
Those silvery con trails in the sky at night

Shadowed

The sun was darkened by a jet airplane
Flying over head
Of all the places it could fly
Of all the spaces it could go
It flew between the sun and me
From point A to point B
There I was
Right time right place
Shadowed by fuselage and wings
As fast as could be
The sun was blackened by a jet airplane
Flying right over me.

Pacifica, California

Ocean breezes
Crashing surf teases
And the fault presses in

Birds flutter and cats mutter
Whales and porpoises grin

With what do the pelicans share?
Airbus and Boeings up in the air
From SFO long journeys begin

It's cloudy and gray
With fog out over the bay
But soon might roll in again

Still gray or blue
No matter the hue
Pacifica has reeled me in

Slow Pass

Passing pass
        Get past me
Get on your merry way
Cruising down the interstate
        Not fast enough to pass
In a timely fashion
Cruising in my blind spot
        Thought you'd pass
But now you're not
So pass me
Press the gas
Get past me
        And hurry on your way

Texas Plains

Part 1:

Fields of cotton
Fluffy and white
Growing in Texas' blood-red soil
Fields of cotton
Neighboring corn
Atop reservoirs of oil
Across the Texas plain
Pumpjacks beget strange scarecrows
But whatever
Encouraged by Texas rain
As long as the crop grows

Part 2:

Pumpjacks turning
Constantly churning
Bringing forth crude oil
All night they turn
All day they churn
Through morn and dusk they toil
Pumpjacks rocking
Squeaking and talking
Pumpjacks on the Texas plain
Pumpjacks working
With faces smirking
Through the snow and the wind and the rain

Roswell, New Mexico

It's not logical, but it's the way that it is in Roswell.
Quirky little town waiting for little green men.
Or are they grays?

"We've come to see the place to be
When you're from another planet."
Quirky little Roswell.
Aliens- green or gray- may come again one day,
they say.

Roswell, Roswell, down under the mystic sky
Come and visit and stay then all will be well.
Our special visitors from afar, in ships that look like
saucers, we receive you enthusiastically.
They say one crashed here one day.
Or was it some 70 miles away?

Whimsical little Roswell.
Strangeness central.
I like it here in Roswell.
I think may belong.
You should come to Roswell
I believe.

California Hills

I love the California hills
All rolli-polli
Plain
With nothing on them
But tan-colored grass
And greenery nudged
Within crags and keeps
Between rolling peaks
Motoring down the five
Sun to the west
I love the California hills
East of SF

One Stormy Night In Seoul

Seoul fidgets sluggishly under sheets of falling water
Jagged lights flash brightly across a secret sky
Rumbling out tales of old while they play among the clouds

Meanwhile, in the streets...
Drivers reign their Kias, Daweoos
Hyundais, Mercedes and Chevys
Tussling for prime jockey positions
Impatiently waiting for a lighted release
Go green, go green
Indifferent to the spectacle playing out above
But annoyed by it nonetheless

But the few watching from behind panes of glass
Sandwiched between streaks of water on one side
And by inert and sullen stares on the other

Until a flash and then crash of lightning
Brings forth a golden smile
Widening as the rumble continues and fades

I feel present, infinite, clued-in to a secret
This night of rain and lightning and thunder
Clears the air, soothes the mind, feeds the spirit
Stay longer my stormy friend
Don't go

Good night

Lima

The streets are patchworks: blocks of stone, concrete and glass.
Cars old and new rush by and hiss as they pass.
The roads are slender, dusty, and askew.
Passersby on sidewalks, saunter 2 by 2.
Some hand in hand, woman and man.
A mother and daughter wearing shirts from Japan.
Gatos pad gently prospecting for scraps.
Poor things, shooed away by elders in hats.
Cloud-heavy skies suffuse a gray hue.
Former Incans of old, now residents of Lima, Peru.

First Night In Rio

Last night was my first night in Rio
In a room on the 22nd floor I slept
With the door to the patio ajar
It was on the beach
With waves and breeze
A lullaby
To sleep and dream of you

We were in a land far away
Other friends of mine were there
No one you know
We were holding hands
It felt ever so special

When the time came to wake up
Hearing the waves hit the beach
And rubbing the sand from my eyes
You were no longer with me
Holding onto my hand
I wish it weren't a dream
Recurring day and night

My first night in Rio
Feeling sad, lonely and missing you

The Sky

    The sky
Amazingly blue punctuated by billowy white clouds
  more grand than a mountain range
Westward flowing behemoths floating
      Growing, morphing, blowing

    The sky
An infinite cathedral of wonder ascends over the blue
  waters of the Caribbean Sea
Soft undulations with white-cap tops
      Jumps, swells, chops

  The sky
Under which an island lurks with rocky sandstone cliffs
 and green vegetation on top
Folks enjoying sandy beaches off the bay
  Splashing, frolicking, at play

  The sky
Unbounded source of inspiration while at sea on this
 essential cruise ship vacation
On deck poolside lounging with pen and paper inking
  Flotation, relaxation, rum drinking

Panama Canal Passage

We entered the Panama Canal waterway under gray sky conditions. It was cooler than expected, breezy, overcast, occasional showers.

A larger ship transporting cargo entered the canal to port, whose curious workers were all on deck spectating our cruise ship and its passengers waving from the decks, "hello!"

Our lock doors opened, we edged ahead with about a foot of clearance on either side of the vessel, from what I could tell. It was certainly a tight fit for our ship, a compliment to her designers with this very canal in mind.

There were four elder passengers seated near me in a lounge on an upper deck also ogling the view and animated over the spectacles of the cargo ship, the tight fit, and our movement through the canal. Except for one.

Mr. Sir, most confident that our ship was motionless, stated, "No, it's them moving, see, we are static."

Immediately catching my attention, I recognized how wrong his assessment was, made more apparent when observing a light post taller than our ship approaching. Unless light posts have acquired the skill to sprout legs and walk, we were moving. Unable to keep silent, I pointed this out, however his selective hearing activated.

I noticed his wife saw the same as I. She beamed to me an intended glance and her eyes said everything I needed to know, 'I suppose my dear husband believes that light posts can move. Please say nothing. It will do no good.'

Returning my gaze out the window, I hear dissent among the ranks, but he reels this in. He ante's up: We. Are. Not. Moving. I next observed him taking note of the light pole, now passing right by our window, and heard a voice of wisdom to this sight from one of the seniors in his party, yet obstinately he continued to ignore it. Not only this, he ups it a notch higher, 'No, that is part of the other ship moving, which makes it appear that we are. But we are not. Our ship is not moving.

Just then, a passing server dressed in the ship's white staff uniform pauses, and with a voice of confidence,
"Hello, Sir, we are moving. The ship, sir. It's moving."

A silence befalls the area as his reeling mind languished in his misguided assessment and getting caught defending it, while his pals know better than to rub it in his face. And when the silence is breached, sheepishly he said, "I stand corrected." While the silence continued, the wife catches my gaze and a smile forms on her wrinkled face that, again, tells me all I need to know...
'See what I have to put up with?'

Sargasso Sea Dreams

Sargassum floating on the Great Sargasso Sea
Sargassum clumps floating past me
The sun is out but soon must set
The moon to shine in your eyes just yet
   Another day passed, another day gone
   Another star to hang your dreams upon
   Dreams of sailing the large ocean blue
   Dreams that one day could easily come true
Not for lack of trying but of getting it done
Some dreams must be carried out while one is still young
So try as you will and will what you might
Wish on dreams to come true on this Sargasso Sea night

Setting Crescent Moon

Setting crescent moon
Riding a bank of fog
To watch this waxing body
Leaves me yet agog

Hanging low
Afloat across the bay
Encouraging a smile
For the night I shall belay

Take me with you please
Your journey through the sky
The best that I can do
Is watch with wishful eye

Seemingly so close
Yet really not at all
As far away as love
When making mortals fall

...

Your beauty is quite powerful
Leaving me possessed
Fantastical eternal
Ornamentally grotesque

Shine me down your beams
Alight and full of silver
Filtered through the fog
With essences to pilfer

Rest now and thank you
Sweet setting crescent moon
I'll look for you tomorrow
Up in the sky at noon

Caterpillar Crossing

Big black
caterpillars
Inching across the highway
Almost as if being pulled by a string
I roll over them and look in my mirrors
To see them either flopping down the road
Head over heels in my car's wake,
Or have become one with my
tires
Sorry little dudes

Big Mountain

        Big mountain
        Rugged and brown
        Queen of the desert sand

    Cut into and dug upon
    Those beastly machines
    Worked by human hand

Big mountain
North of town
You were once most grand

Despoiled; over mined
Brutalized to extinct
A pillager's wonderland

        Oh, Mountain
        Beauty taken
        Antiquated
        Spirit shaken
        Majesty banned

                Wrongfully downcast
                Charmed to the last
                Big mountain
                Damned

Were I A Tree

Tall trees surround and look down on me
I wonder what they say for I am not a tree
For if I were I could speak their tongue
Converse with the old and laugh with the young
I would grow tall so you could have a look around
Climb among my branches, be careful, don't fall down
Pick at my fruit when it's ripe, and oh so sweet
Find in my shade a relaxing cool retreat
I'd sway and dance when the wind comes round
Pray no one comes to chop me down
It would be so neat to be a tree
But I can't so I won't and I'll just be me

I Am The Burning Man

I'm painted in hues you'll never see
I've got grand ideas that'll never be
See the sky reflected in my eyes
May it come as no surprise

I live for the desert's pain
Out of the grinding blacktop mundane
In a vast desert expanse
Easily unnoticed at first glance
In this new home I feel remarkably grand
For here in spirit, full of desire
I'm a worshiped man

So come the end of the day
Seek revelation and find your way
Capture me
Release me
Choose to live
With hearts to give

...

Follow me from here
With intentions of diffraction so clear

Into the sun
I have come
I am the learned man
I am the burning man

All Are Artists

This swirl of sand surrounding me
Makes no sense at all
And the sun tries to reach for me
But I'm already gone

When the night overtakes
The patch of ground I'm on
Flashing lights that encircle me
Will keep me going til the dawn

When you're in this city
Time has no meaning
The labels we've placed
Fall to the floor fatiguing

Black Rock welcomes all
Whether an artist or not contrive
With radical self expression
You're an artist simply being alive

So why keep my eyes closed
When I go astray
'Cause there's nothing worth seeing
That we didn't already create

Dragonflies Surrender

When we're ants on the poppies
And there's no song left in the whirligigs
The dragonflies surrender
      And dish no more
For they are the only ones
Who truly know the score

When we're frogs on the lilies
And there's no babble in the brook
The dragonflies surrender
      And fall to the floor
For they are the only ones
Who know the heart for sure

When we're mist on the prairie
And the sand has left the desert
The dragonflies surrender
      And in the sky no longer soar
For they are the only ones
Who can hear the silent roar

Early Arrival

Pause the engine, this snakes quite a way
Listen for the gong's hypnotic tone
To signal the gates open, time to enter home

Encircled by dust, sight, and love for a week
My annual pilgrimage...I'm home alright
I will dance at will and gyrate late into the night

Hurry the gong for the sun's growing glare
I'm waiting for a slap on the ass
From a girl with green and yellow hair
She's dressed in artistic flair from head to toe
I can feel her heart dance and flutter like a dove
She's a one-woman show

Soon I'll be hugging everyone I meet
There's nothing as sweet as home in the dust
Under a blazing sun in outrageous heat

The stars come together to create community
I love being home in the dessert I love most dear
So sound the gong, I've waited too long
The Man's been Burning all year

I Am

Out in the darkness, the cool air hugs my frame. The night sky is illuminated only by the stars. Oh, and flashing neon and fire. No, I'm not at the scene of an emergency. I am home. In the desert. Dusty. Full of love, compassion, optimism, emotional overload. One week of the year. I am home.

Drums and music, cheers and laughter, dance across the desert floor to where I stand, in the middle of nothing, in the center of the universe. I am surrounded by it all. I am happy.

The neon man stands sentry off in the distance. He watches over us as we revel and slough the fears, concerns and worries that bog us down in the default world of blacktop negativity and fomented fears. He will burn to pave the way for new growth. He is my friend—of this my oath. I am grateful.

I am free, an American, a thinker, a lover, a partyer and an artist.
I am a Burner.
I am a spark that is lighter than air; inspiring and ethereal.
I am home.

To The Shore

I shed my robes
The costume that says I am enslaved by society
It's the end of the week
The start of a month in the middle of a year I'll soon forget
I head to the shore

Between two bays where the water rushes and rumbles
I head to the shore

And the foot of the mountains where the fog presses
tightly
I head to the shore

Another day and my mind might explode
It's time for a chemical restoration
Of this I am sure
To shed fondly for a while my life's precious facade

My champions will be there too
My chosen family
A community
My rock
No more will I feel dead inside
At least not the next 3 days
When I see the colors, three

...

Blue, red, and white.
Where soothing water rushes and rumbles
Calming me with their knavish ways
Grab a fist full of sand
The water washes it clean
The light and the tanned
The beach becomes me

A circle of light borne of the night
And surrounding the fire is a circle of friends
With hearts connected better than our hands
And this circle of life now makes amends

So the time has finally come
I shed these robes and don silly things on my head
And things more silly in my mind
Maybe it's time to loosen myself and be free on the beach
I think it's beyond that time
Head to the shore

Don't look now I'm out the door
Don't look back I'm on the west seventeen
To the jungle on the beach
To the land where my soul roams even when my body's yet at home
To the cows in their pastures above the shore
To the beats in a place we call the jungle
And the crazy beautiful people whom I adore
I head to the shore

Beach Haikus

I know of a place
where my psyche can explore
things it thought were lost

to the jungle flee
for the jungle is happy
and the mind is free

I'm wondering where
I could run to this weekend
and be with my friends

I could fill my arms
my eyes as well as my ears
with the likes of you

the cows are up there
they like to watch us all dance
and wish to join us

cuddle dome night lights
will illuminate the way
so please come 'round soon

The Jungle

A place where the waves crash upon the shore
Where water grinds rock into a sandy floor
Back in the vegetation allure
I appear again

A 3-sided swing is built in the sea breeze haze
The stage is set and lit ablaze
I appear again

We'll be treated like honey and fed if we crave
And when we are thirsty we'll drink sans delay
Our body shall they comfort when feeling out of reach
I remember a jungle around the corner on the beach

It filled my soul and gave me peace
Littered with neon and cracked laughter
And no sound but the beating heart increased
And the rhythm of the gathered gods hereafter

Firelight

The beach at night is too dark to find me
So follow the firelight and my visage is the smoke
I am the roar of the beauty there
Search the surf and find me in the waves
The waves keeping time moving to and fro
Holding the beat in my heart
My heart keeps beat to the freaky rhythm
And the rhythm thrives from the skills of the DJ
So I look around in the firelight
To regain my friends there in bewitching smoke
The dark is our rite in the cool air on the shore
We miss the ones who aren't there
Our chosen family as close as the next song
The jungle can never contain me
Stand aside and let me be
I am the beauty that dances
Magical things surrounding me
Find the crevasse and fill me within
For I am light
The means to an end
The world will ever be the same again
On our rock
An island
On the shore
In the firelight

Pulse And Blend

The lights wash over me
Whirling lights bathe and cleanse
Pulse and blend
See the lights washing over me

The bass pulses within me
Pushes through my veins
Pulse and blend
Feel the bass pulsing within

The drums beat my heart
Dances with my soul
Pulse and blend
Listen to the drums beat, beat, beat away

Spiral around
Upon the ground
And come together
In a most sensual way
Look at all it's doing for you
There's a party at the speaker
Is this a party for two?

Handfast On The Mountain

Handfasting couple dominate their world on a mountainside that slopes both gently, and with solid intent, towards the river in the valley, along with their friends in bright colors, who are both scantily and sky clad, moving to happy beats spinning on the decks, amplified with love, for all of the passion flowing among those encircling the bride and groom, who glow as bright as the nearby burn barrels to keep us warm, on the sides of which are torched-out figures and letters that speak in tongues of sparks, flying into the skies which slowly lower with fog as the celebrants all begin to twist, spin, hop, and gyrate to those lovely beats from the DJ into the early morn.

> We don't need a raver here
> We got more DJs on our mountain
> On top of the world
> Sure hope the beats keep with the handfast
> Come and gather, my friends
> Circle around the bride and the groom
> Let's party this mountain down
> Let us light this mountain up with loving flames
> From hoops and burn barrels
> From staff and chains
> Let's light this mountain up
> Until the river runs dry
> We won't stop until the light of day
> Let our joy lift the fog into the sky

Outback

I've had it with the city and must go north. Past Petaluma, left at Cotati. Out past Sebastipol.
There, the redwoods embrace me- awoken from slumber they happily befriend. A thousand years and it's like I'm home.
Bliss.
Transcend.
Across the creek, into the woods for just a night or three.
Everything unwanted melts away.
    I'm loved.
        I'm sane.
           I'm high.
We'll dance under the moonlight and laugh by the fireside. Fly like flags with thanks to the Skaggs. Now pack your bags with tasty goods and ready the night.
North and across the creek in the magical redwoods.

Love Is A Gift

I had a dream that I was floating in the sea.
No, it was the desert.
There were sleeping giants, or were they dead?
Covered in rocks and small shrubs.
Perhaps they came here to die.
Perhaps they came to watch over me.

I was a part of something larger than life
I could not adequately see.
It surrounded me, encompassed me, it embraced me.
And in some ways it ate me up and spat me out.
But mostly it filled me. It occupied my sensibilities with passion and a deep need to better understand things around me.
                Politics.
        Mechanics.   Science.
            Love.
            Humanity
I floated down to the dusty surface and met a woman who brought me a flower.
A man who embraced me.
A child, who offered a drink, then squeezed my
            …

hand and carried me through the night.
I found things I thought had died. I lost things I thought would always haunt me.
And I smiled.
I tried to give back, but felt I had nothing equal to that which I had already received.
With little to give, instead I sparkled.
And they told me,
Brother, LOVE is a gift.

<u>Bright</u>

                I miss you so much when I'm having fun
Nothing fades you from my life

I Couldn't If I Tried

I'm glad to see that after all
this time

You still do it to me like no
one else

Since our first kiss I fell into
you

And I never climbed back
out

Least Expected

The buttons of my shirt came undone with ease
Under a magic touch, your fingers a treat
You sought heat on a night that felt cold
We added passion to the bonfire that starry night
Unsure as to how, but the taste was so sweet

A tease outrageous from days ago until now
Is this possible?
Love strikes when we are at our weakest
Most cruel
A fragile adversary from such an unjust assault am I

I would travel the world over to see us there infinitely
This sight shall never pale as the sun shades me from you
Happiness is found in many corners of the world
Eternally happy returning home to you

Erred Retention

I went back to where we met
Funny how time stalled
Was much smaller than thought was true
Like going back to times of youth
Where ways once grandiose become petty
Memories now of dust and a bit cobwebby

I went back to where we met
The first time I fell in love
Cupid's arrow shot from above

I went back to where we met
To the beginning
We were happy and spinning
In love at first sight
Passion with improbable might

I went back to where we first met
And was swept away
Under the rainbow
A dazzling light bouquet
How we are still happy and spinning
Only our memory thinning

Honeyed Heart

Normally my heart is strong and extols songs of joy to my soul

But when it comes to you my heart grows weak, sappy and sweet

But You're Always In My Heart

       If you could be here now
In paradise with me
Sound of waves crashing the shore

       If only you were present right now
Under this banyan tree
On my beach I so adore

       I'd hang our love on every bough
A display of our heart's rapport

       If you were with me now
Holding my hand
Words of adoration drawn in sand
My soul's sacred ore

       If only you were able to hear this vow
I'd be the happiest man
Forevermore

Ode To A Friend

There are so many things said to a friend.
Complex feelings of our solidarity are difficult to
accurately express.
Since we've known one another,
You've known what to do and
Exactly how to be:
Silent when you're needed,
Strong when I'm weak,
Sober and comforting when the world seems so bleak.
You bring me down when I'm too high,
And lift me up when you see me cry.
Yes. You've known how to be;
Exactly what to do;
And when you're in need of help you allow me to care for
you.
So permit me an offer, just one meaningful thing,
In hopes to enlighten you of my motive
Loyalty:
heartfelt, uncompromising and without conditions.
The real deal.
My friendship.

Strange The Power

Strange that I lie here thinking
About what keeps me up at night
Gives me such an odd feeling
Not knowing what's wrong or right

There's a stranger looking through the window
Trying to get in from the pain
With an otherworldly look in his eye
I try to hide but I cannot look away

Go on he says, just go and leave me
You face the cold but can't face the wind
He hopes to watch me turn and walk
But ignores the power of a friend

Strange what loss can do to a man
And the years that pass still hang on
Strange how I linger in this dark space
To help a mind that I fear has gone

I remember the day we first met
A day when my heart took the lead
There's a day I remember better yet
To help a friend who has been deceived

After all this time I still find it strange
How you are unwilling to take my hand
These rippled panes I can barely see through
I'd sooner break to get to you

Muse Gratitude

I love writing when the Muse strikes.
Sometimes the flow is slow. I stop and think, what line is next. What rhyme...I'm vexed. Even with all my bits of papers and notes of text.
Not this time. This one came out as fast as I could write. Inspired by you, my inspirational muse.
Sometimes I guard my feelings and write in code. Not this time. Just let it flow.
Often, I write what I know. From the heart. With my soul. With gratitude. She lights the fuse. Thanks to my creative muse.

Haiku For Two

you always climb down
the pedestal made for you
eggshell pedestal

the west coast I'm bound
I love the way the sun sets
nights along the beach

right beside the sea
the food was impeccable
hot tub melted me

I'm falling faster
he found me, I was alone
and I've passed the moon

Revisit

I'll go back again some day
        To see how things have changed
                And I can't help but wonder
                      If I'll still see that smile

The Little Things

Old man sitting in an old chair
on an old porch in front of an old house in the older part of town.
I walked by and paid him no mind- until he said hello.
"Hi," I replied back and met his smile with one of my own.
He bade me to have a good evening. I looked back and said,
"I hope you have a good one, too."
He looked so happy that someone spoke to him. As if
he had been ignored for some time.
I was happy he spoke to me. He made my day, that
strange old man in good cheer.
I passed the house the other day. The chair was gone and
there was nothing inside.
I think he died so I shed a tear.

Zebraback Rider

Today I saw a zebra
A black and white striped horse
Upon which sat a woman wearing balloons
                    I am certain it was a woman
For all the balloons obscured the rider under them
Green, pink, yellow, red, gold, and orange balloons.
      She rode it side saddle
            In pink leggings real tight
      Riding out of a jungle
Into a clearing so near
Today I saw a zebra
      Just an everyday thing, of course

Haiku: A Poem Of Seventeen Syllables In 3 Lines Of 5, 7, 5

a Haiku each day
January, all month long
join me if you can

monsters surround me
I see them and laugh at them
I'm a monster, too

nobody likes you
very sad but also true
and, you are ugly

don't come around here
will you please stay far away?
go on now, git!

I lost my baby
in a big crowd of people
let's go have some fun

Santa is an ass
no, not Santa, but Satan
dyslexia sucks

Sisters

Sister on the left of me
Smart inspiration

Sister on the right
Defies explanation

Such warmth
Both aglow
Get ready
Let's go

Battle of smarts
Battle of wills
Internally guarding demonstrative feels

She's terse
She's wit
She versed
Such grit

But at the day's overdue end
They toast one another- an honorable friend

January Haiku Challenge

just ten more Haikus
and then my month will be done
so please enjoy these

a birthday for some
with cake and surprises, too
have fun getting old

a plane in the sky
a bird pooped in my right eye
maybe that's no plane

Thai food in Thai Town
my favorite pad se ew
too spicy to eat

off to see my sweet
a rose for the one I love
asked if I brought beer

going on a date
no dinner reservation.
do you like fast food?

...

your eyes enthrall me
I could stare at them all night
were they brown or blue?

a flame flickering
illuminates the night sky
it burns just for you

the moon that shines down
shines on both you and on me
stop hogging my moon

all week go, go, go
thank goodness for the weekend
now to start my chores

your hand, it trembles
much as does my heart for you
since you hold it so

it's either you or
I spend the rest of my life
alone by myself

I know that was twelve
why are you counting along?
mind your own business

Bowl Of Oranges

Climbed to the top, you did.
Representing the group, I see.
Sat there in judgment everyone and me.

Those eyes intense. Those lips puckered.
Full of yourself.
Palpable. Or, might I say pulpable?
So funny I eat it up.

Why would you be shocked? You're an orange.

Bonus Haikus:

an orange with big eyes
staring at me intently
and then I ate him

don't judge me Sir Orange
thinking you're safe in that bowl
how could this happen?

Aw Shucks

Oysters on the half shell.
They're not all that bizarre.
You know that they're in season
In months spelled with an R.

I like my red sauce spicy.
Pass the horseradish, if you please.
I eat them with a cracker.
Give that lemon wedge a squeeze.

I can eat them by the dozen.
Wash them down with cold beer.
Oysters on the half shell.
They're so good this time of year.

She Asked Me To Talk Biscuit Pie Crusts

Delicious biscuit pie crusts
This talk is sure a must
Be it for pecan or cherry
Chocolate silk or even blueberry
Let's sit and have a chat
Does this crust make my ass look fat?
Oh, I do so love to talk about pie
On this topic I shall never lie
So let's discuss a crust made of biscuit dough
The best pie crust you will ever know

My Grandfather's Robe

Grandfather's robe was gifted to me
The day we laid him to rest
I would have accepted most anything
It was embraced at my grandma's behest
In patterns of old in tan and red
I cherished what he had once worn
My grandfather was much smaller than me
Which then left me feeling forlorn

Funny how things when one is young
Shrink so much as we age
My grandfather always appeared so large
To me he was evermore sage

The thought of him that came to mind
As I first tried my newfound robe on
How had this man that I so loved
Lost so much of his benevolent brawn
This was the robe of a smaller man
Someone much smaller than me
I knew from the moment I put it on
Placing my arm down the sleeve

While I was initially able to don his robe
It was certainly too tight to wear
It barely fastened over my front
When raising my arms it might tear
But this robe was mine now, I'll tell you what
The size of it I didn't care

I kept this robe forever, I did
Took it with me each time I moved
From one closet then to the next
It stayed with me very unused
But much like as with his other effects
This tribute to him be surely approved

Then thirty-six years past his death
I became frightfully ill
Within the first month I lost twenty pounds
Recovering, I lost further body weight still

And then one day, a hundred pounds lighter
I thought inquisitively
I went to my closet, all the way back
Had a moment I couldn't believe
For the very first time since the robe became mine
Would you believe it finally fits
My arms felt right within the sleeve
Extra room for each of my pits

It fit all the way around my girth
With lots of material to spare
I tied it majestically with the sash
And now it is ready to wear

I'm pleased with myself for rising above
To loose all the weight that I did
But one thing I'm notably gleeful of
Is wearing Pa's robe for the very first time
Since owning it as his grand kid

Disclosure

My demons whisper things to me
                         Softly in my ears

They are quite intent to fill my head
> With crazy idears

APPENDIX OF POEMS
And background information
Cover art by Penguin Scott in Pasadena, California

Page: Title:

5   **Mother's Day 2014** I often wrote Mom poems for even the smallest reasons. I rarely kept a copy, since they were usually written on cards or notes I'd hide around the house for her to find. This may have been the year we found out she had cancer. It made sense to use it in this book's dedication.

7   **Seven** written in 1996 is a true tale from my days at Southampton Montessori School in Houston. So many special memories of my time there in K and 1st grade.

9   **Snoopykins** from 1987 when going to Corpus to visit my grandparents and meeting Buffy after Snoopy died. Snoopy and Buffy are the only 2 pets I recall my grandparents owning.

10 **Lampasas, Texas on a Hot Afternoon** written in 2009, after a trip there to visit the family grave site. I know little about my paternal family but was curious where my great grandfather may have lived.

12 **Memories** written in 2003 based on actual memories I have from when I was 3 or 4. Mom was always amazed that I had memories from that young.

13 **Corpus, Back in the Day** written in 1993 after a visit to see Memaw and asking about her memories of Paw, as I motioned to his photo on the wall. She told me she had few memories of 'that man,' only that they had been married. Mortally wounded me, figuratively.

15 **Grandmother** was written in 2017 after my Maternal Grandmother turned 90. I altered the end for this publication.

16 **Memorial Day** written in 2017, after visiting my grandfather's grave site on Memorial Day.

18 **Borger** written in 2007 after my close friend, Martha Allison, passed. A neighbor of my grandparents, she was a 2nd grandmother to me. I grew up going to Borger for long stints starting around the age of 3. It's as much home to me as Houston.

20 **Like Mom Used to Do** was written in 1997 after a bad day and realizing that I sought comfort doing things I recall Mom doing and recognizing the pattern I inherited.

22 **Turkey Talk** written in 2020 for the first Thanksgiving without Mom. How could I forget a story like that?

24 **A Day for Mom** written circa 2015. Found this in my hundreds of poetry notes. Thanks for indulging me.

25 **Twenty Years Later** written for the 20th anniversary of 9/11/01.

26 **Challenger** written in 2022 after learning that they now think the 7 were alive when the Challenger crew compartment hit the water. I was a senior in high school when Challenger exploded.

27 **Through the Salt** written in 2004 while living in South San Francisco.

28 **Grief** written in 2010 after the death of my familiar, Adelie.

29 **Mary** written in 2019 following the death of my best friend and confidante.

30 **Redwoods** written in 2019 following the death of another dear friend. 2019 sucked for me.

31 **Falling** written 2009 and is mostly true.

32 **Delicate Web** written 2014.

33 **Low Priority** written in 2013.

34	**Adjust** written in 1997 during a prolific time of my poetry writing when living in Annapolis. I'd stay up late drinking and penning.
35	**Filbert's Tapping** written in 2011 about a bird I named because it would tap every day for 2 summers in a row.
36	**Needing Sad Songs** written in 2021.
37	**Cede** written 1990, a period of my life when I felt lost.
38	**Spring** written 2000.
39	**Dream Journal** written 2006. I've kept these off and on throughout the years. They may become another book of poetry.
40	**On the Mountainside** a true tale written 2003.
41	**Through the Window** written 1999.
43	**Ohma Gods** written in 1997, was one of Mom's favorites.
45	**Special** written in 1997. There are so many people this could be about. If we met after 1997, you're safe.
47	**Candidate** written in 2016. Go figure.
49	**Travel Lust** written in 1996, when I first began using this title. I traveled often as general manager of the Harley dealership. The 2nd and 3rd stanzas were written in 2006 and the four combined for this book.
50	**Annapolis** written in 2012. My town home was 50 feet from the Severn River with views of the Naval Academy and the capitol dome.
51	**Leaving California** written in 2014 while driving to Texas after transferring to Houston.
52	**Planes in Clouds** written 1999.
53	**Metal Birds** written in 1989. Testament to having airplane disease (travel lust) since little.
54	**Con Trails at Night** written in 2014.
55	**Shadowed** written 1987. In the early 70s, we lived under the flight path of Hobby Airport and I always thrilled when getting shadowed by a plane.
56	**Pacifica, California** written 2009 shortly after moving there.
57	**Slow Pass** written in 1986 driving between Houston, Corpus, and Dallas.
58	**Texas Plains** Part 1 written in 2014 and Part 2 written 1988.
60	**Roswell, New Mexico** written 2014, after spending a few hours there on my drive to Texas.
61	**California Hills** written on my drive back to Houston, 2014.
62	**One Stormy Night in Seoul** written 2012 about a layover in S. Korea.
64	**Lima** one of my favorite destinations, written in 2015 after numerous layovers there.
65	**First Night in Rio** written 2017.
66	**The Sky** written on a cruise vacation in 2005.
68	**Panama Canal Passage** a true tale written in 2015.
70	**Sargasso Sea Dreams** written in 2016 while in the Sargasso Sea.
71	**Setting Crescent Moon** if you read my book, *What About the Bees,* you know of the poems inspired by the photos posted on line by my friend, Bruce Wismer. This is one of those, circa 2015.
73	**Caterpillar Crossing** after miles of road, I realized the little black things were caterpillars. I stopped to say hello to one. Many were harmed in the making of this poem. So sorry.
74	**Big Mountain** on my drive to Texas in 2014, was this mountain in California that was being obliterated by mining.
76	**Were I a Tree** one of numerous poems I wrote under a banyan tree on a layover in Hawaii, 2017.

77	**I am the Burning Man** written 2005 during the time I was going to Burning Man each Fall. This was the largest outdoor arts festival in the world (and may still be) and it changed my life in numerous and profoundly positive ways.
79	**All Are Artists** written 2005. Burning Man opened my life to a rich social life of artists of all walks of life. Many are still close friends of mine.
80	**Dragonflies Surrender** written in 2006 after seeing a few in the dessert. All my life, dragonflies have been kind to me, often landing on me to say hello.
81	**Early Arrival** written 2007, the final year I attended (and graduated) Burning Man, and the only year I didn't have early access. Waiting in line for the gates to open was a new experience.
82	**I Am** written in 2002 on the Playa, what Burners call the land on which the city of Black Rock sits for only a few weeks each year. A big, dusty desert.
83	**To the Shore** written 2007 after befriending a group of fun people who gathered once a month to camp, rave, party, and share.
85	**Beach Haikus** written between 2006 and 2009. I've always loved writing Haikus and discovered a few fans of the form at the beach.
86	**The Jungle** referencing a private section of the beach beyond the parking lot that was shaded by cliffs and vegetation, which we called the jungle. It wasn't an actual jungle. 2008
87	**Firelight** written in 2006 about going to the beach with my friends.
88	**Pulse and Blend** originally written in 1989, but I added the final 2 lines for this book, as inspired by a friend of mine known to party in front of the speaker. (Yes, you, Dirt Girl.)
89	**Handfast on the Mountain** written circa 2011. After the beach events stopped, a friend, Heidi, hosted "That thing on the mountain," One year she got married during our annual pilgrimage to Northern California.
90	**Outback** written in 2012 after the beach events ceased, we began camping at Outback, in Guerneville, CA. The Skaggs owned and ran the camp ground and became friends. Michael is like a brother and Tracie is abreeze in the redwood trees.
91	**Love is a Gift** inspired by my trips to Burning Man, written in 2004.
93	**Bright** written in 2014 on the beach in Maui and seeing whales off shore.
94	**I Couldn't if I Tried** written in 1986 in tribute to the love my grandparents had for each other.
95	**Least Expected** inspired by a true event in 2013.
96	**Erred Retention** written 2019.
97	**Honeyed Heart** written 2000 in Annapolis.
98	**But You're Always in my Heart** written 2017 under a banyan tree in Hawaii.
99	**Ode to a Friend** written in 2006.
100	**Strange the Power** written in 1989.
102	**Muse Gratitude** written 2013. So many times I finish writing and wonder, where the hell did that come from? Experiences I've never had, words I don't normally use, often, an image of a word that I don't know until I look it up. The only way I can explain it is that I'm being used as a vessel. I'm happy to oblige.
103	**Haiku for Two** found loose in my notes, about someone I know. Circa 2019.
104	**Revisit** written 1995 when I moved to Annapolis.
105	**The Little Things** a true tale written in 2022.
106	**Zebraback Rider** written 2020 from a photo in a magazine.

107	**Haiku: A Poem...** an actual challenge I put forth on social media, found in my notes. I cannot recall the year, but either circa 2013 or 2015.
108	**Sisters** written in 2015 and inspired by reality.
109	**January Haiku Challenge** on a separate note from those found on page 107 were these.
111	**Bowl of Oranges and Bonus Haiku** written in 2020 when visiting my brother and family. I secretly placed google eyes around the house, including on an orange on the breakfast table. The next day, forgetting I had done so, it made me laugh.
112	**Aw Shucks** written on my way to satisfy an oyster craving in 2021.
113	**She Asked me to Talk Biscuit Pie Crusts** written 2015 and inspired by Sweet Mary.
114	**My Grandfather's Robe** a true story about Paw, written in 2023.
116	**Disclosure** written in 2002.

Other works by Penguin Scott:

◊ **"Upon the Hues of Sunset"** – A little more philosophical, with poetry on heartbreak, as well as uplifting works on travel and falling in love.

◊ **"What About the Bees"** – Light humor and imaginative topics that includes themes of growing up, heartbreak and current affairs.

Coming soon:

Penguin's, "Travel Lust" a series of novels about his travels as a flight attendant.

ABOUT THE AUTHOR

Penguin Scott was born and raised in Texas. He grew up in Houston and moved between there and Dallas several times. He began writing poetry in high school when he lived in Dallas. Penguin didn't get serious about poetry until college in the late 1980s, at the University of Houston, where he studied creative writing. He would eventually live on all three US coasts.

During the early and mid 1990s, Penguin joined the performance company at the Texas Renaissance Festival in Houston. This period of creativity encouraged him to hone the writing talents he developed in college.

In 1995 he moved to Annapolis, MD when purchasing a Harley-Davidson dealership with his father. He credits this difficult period of his life, being away from family and the stress of working alongside his father, as being the inspiration for one of his most prolific periods of writing. It was during this period he earned the nickname Penguin, based on his collection of penguin items—at one time the largest collection in the USA.

In 2000, Penguin left Annapolis for San Francisco, taking a job with a major airline. His travel lust spawned many travel poems during the 2000s. Living in the San Francisco Bay Area for 14 years introduced him to various artistic influences. He attended Burning Man, the world's largest outdoor arts festival and showcase for radical self-expression, for seven years (2001 to 2007).

This led to an expanded social circle of fellow "burners," a cohesive and colorful group of friends who would come together for monthly camp outs on the beach, for what was essentially 48-hour raves with a bent on artistic creativity. Many poems were written on this beach, and an area known as The Jungle.

In 2014, Penguin transferred and moved back to Texas to spend time caring for his maternal grandmother. Considered the leading ladies of his life, she and Penguin's mother were among his biggest fans of his writing and poetry, encouraging his expanding talents.

In 2017, Penguin rediscovered his poetry notes, that when combined, formed a stack of papers over a foot high. He began pouring through them to cull his favorites and flesh out some that were unfinished. The collection showcased in this series of three books, released in 2023, are only a small portion of what he has written since the mid 1980s. Surely, more will follow.

In the span of five years, Penguin lost his father, mother and grandmother, as well as several dear friends and other family. Additionally, he contracted the Corona Virus in December, 2020, and is still struggling with Post Covid conditions that affects his cognitive skills, preventing him from fulfilling his role as a safety a professional with the airline. At least temporarily.

If you've enjoyed this book, please buy more copies—they make great gifts. If you wish to purchase an autographed copy or donate to the PenguinScott Post Covid Fund, contact him directly. Penguin Scott accepts Paypal donations at the email address below.

Penguin Scott can be reached as indicated here:

penguinscott.com
authorpenguinscott@gmail.com